THE BEST OF EVA CASSIDY

PIANO VOCAL GUITAR

INTRODUCTION

BY HUGH CASSIDY, EVA'S FATHER

If you have acquired this songbook, you are no doubt a fan of Eva Cassidy – her voice and her music. This songbook exemplifies the music Eva chose to sing and play on her guitar. Eva was not a songwriter, but rather chose to sing songs that touched her deeply. Her arrangements of popular American, English and traditional music have become classic interpretations of the 21st Century.

Eva was born in 1963 and died of cancer in 1996. In her short 33 years, she absorbed the music which she learned as a child, as a teenager and a young adult. She put her own spin on many classic melodies and made them her own. This songbook offers you a wide array of songs, all arranged by Eva. Hers is the ultimate compliment to the songsmiths of her own and previous generations.

Eva first learned guitar chords from me when she was barely nine years old. I was then working as a bass player and guitarist in order to supplement the family's income. Eva, the third child in our family of four children, loved group singing for family holidays and special occasions. She created and sang wonderful harmonies in the back seat of the car on family outings as a very young child. Both Eva and her brother Dan were born with an ability to grasp sound, melody and harmony.

Now we know that Eva was very much influenced by the family record collection which included LPs by Pete Seeger, Buffy Saint Marie and Ray Charles, just to name a few. Thanks in part to this early exposure, Eva learned the melodies and rhythm of folk, blues and jazz. In high school, she was involved with other young people who had a sincere interest in music. Given that Eva was born in 1963, and her friends favoured rock, Eva participated in a high school and college rock band called 'Stonehenge'. Always, however, Eva worked on her own perfecting her ballads. She created her unique arrangement of *Over The Rainbow* and recorded it on a home tape recorder as early as 1984. At that time Eva was 21 years old. Many of the songs included in this book were arranged by her during her teenage years and twenties.

Songs which Eva learned to play and sing with the family include Pete Seeger's *How Can I Keep From Singing?* and Harold Arlen's *Over The Rainbow*. Eva and her siblings adored the movie, *Wizard Of Oz*, and Eva loved *Over The Rainbow* from the time she was a child. During high school she developed her versions of *Stormy Monday* and *Wade In The Water*. *Do, Lord*, now called *Way Beyond The Blue*, was a tune which our family sang together in four-part harmony from the time Eva was about 10 years old.

In 1992, Eva recorded a CD entitled *The Other Side*, sharing the bill with Chuck Brown, the 'Father Of Go-Go'. From that album we include *Dark End Of The Street* and *Need Your Love*.

Live At Blues Alley was Eva's first solo album, recorded and released in 1996. From that album we include her versions of *Fields of Gold*, *Wonderful World* and *People Get Ready*.

Following Eva's death on November 2nd 1996, her second solo album entitled *Eva By Heart* was released. From that album we have selected Eva's versions of *Blues In The Night* and *Songbird*.

Posthumously, her mother and I signed a national/international recording contract with Blix Street Records. Blix Street created the CD *Songbird* which has become a million seller. That was quickly followed by *Time After Time*. From *Time After Time* we have chosen the following songs: *Ain't No Sunshine*, *Kathy's Song*, *At Last* and the title tune *Time After Time*.

Eva's family and friends so much enjoyed her as a person and as a musical talent during her lifetime. We laughed with her and cried with her and enjoyed every opportunity to hear her perform in small clubs and at our family gatherings. It is now so gratifying that the world has come to hear and appreciate the Eva whom we knew and loved.

I know that there are other music lovers out there who have the talent and the interest to play and use the wonderful songs in this book and to experience the joy with which Eva executed each song.

I never fully understood Eva's attraction to certain songs. In retrospect, I know that she not only had a God-given talent in her voice but also a rare ability to select wonderful material. I may have provided the early instruction and guidance, but Eva was very self-possessed and determined in her selection and interpretation of musical material. She picked 'the best' and so, we call this songbook *The Best Of Eva Cassidy*. We, her family and close friends, invite you to enjoy the music Eva loved.

Best Wishes

HUGH CASSIDY

THE BEST OF EVA CASSIDY

PIANO VOCAL GUITAR

PUBLISHED 2002
© INTERNATIONAL MUSIC PUBLICATIONS LTD
GRIFFIN HOUSE 161 HAMMERSMITH ROAD LONDON W6 8BS ENGLAND

PRODUCTION ANNA JOYCE
DESIGN DOMINIC BROOKMAN
MUSIC ARRANGED BY BARNES MUSIC ENGRAVING

AIN'T NO SUNSHINE

Words and Music by
Bill Withers

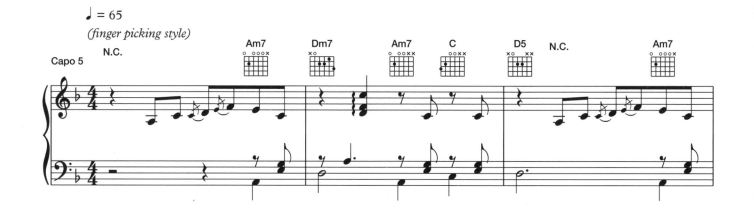

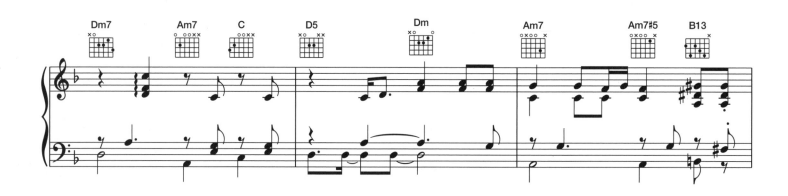

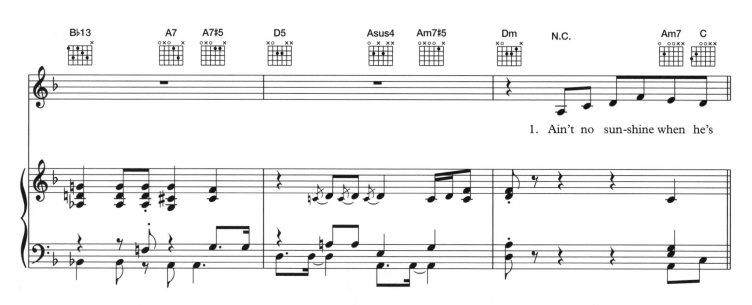

1. Ain't no sun-shine when he's

Well I know, I know, I know, I know, I know, I know, I know, I know, I___ know,

AT LAST

Words by Mack Gordon
Music by Harry Warren

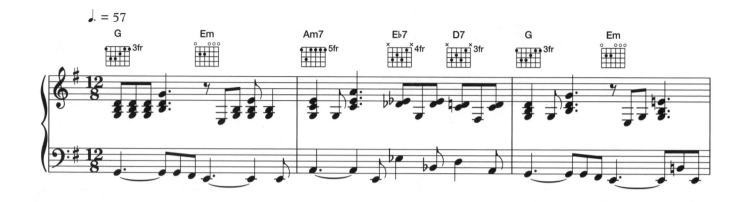

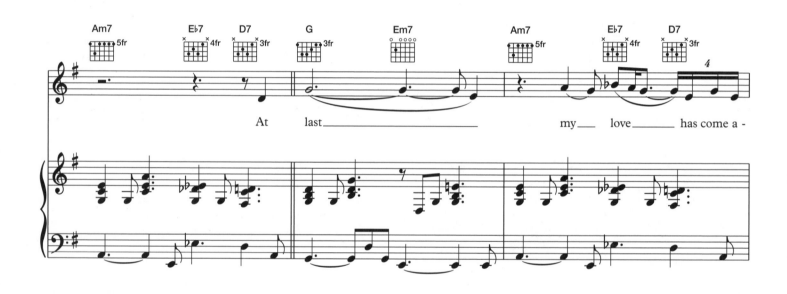

At last_____ my__ love_____ has come a -

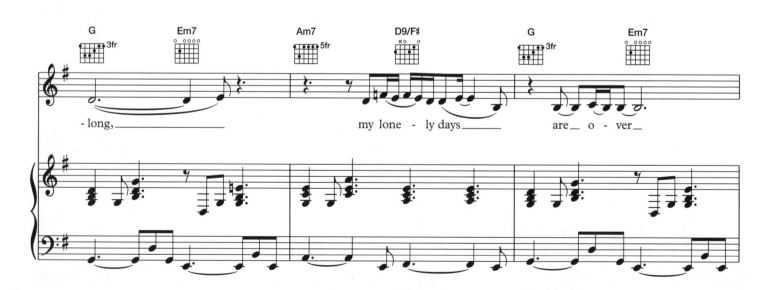

-long,_____ my lone - ly days_____ are o - ver_

AUTUMN LEAVES

Words by Jacques Prevert
Music by Joseph Kosma
English Translation by Johnny Mercer

au-tumn leaves ___ start ___ to fall.

Since ___

BLUE SKIES

Words and Music by
Irving Berlin

BLUES IN THE NIGHT

Words by Johnny Mercer
Music by Harold Arlen

DARK END OF THE STREET

Words and Music by
Chips Moman and Dan Penn

1. At the dark end___ of the street, that's where___ we al - ways

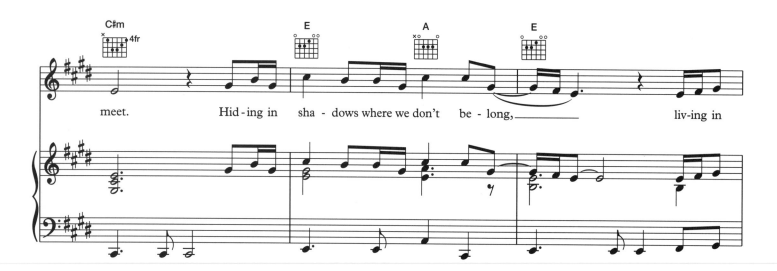

meet. Hid-ing in sha - dows where we don't be - long,_____ liv-ing in

dark-ness to hide_____ our wrong. You and me at the

EASY STREET DREAM

Words and Music by
Steven Digman

1. It's Sun - day morn - ing,_____
2. It was on - ly for plea - sure,___ our

I can feel__ the side__ ef - fects,___ when you shake out your bo - dy
love_____ took a back - seat,___ my__ heart_ went cra - zy and my

FIELDS OF GOLD

Words and Music by
Gordon Sumner

HOW CAN I KEEP FROM SINGING?

Words Traditional
Music by Ira Sankey
Arranged by Eva Cassidy

NEED YOUR LOVE SO BAD

Words and Music by
John Mertis Jr

KATHY'S SONG

Words and Music by
Paul Simon

1. I hear the driz - zle of the rain,

3. And as I watch the drops of rain,

weave their wea - ry paths

OVER THE RAINBOW

Words by E Y Harburg
Music by Harold Arlen

PEOPLE GET READY

Words and Music by
Curtis Mayfield

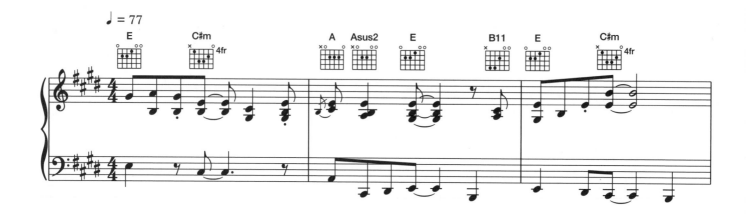

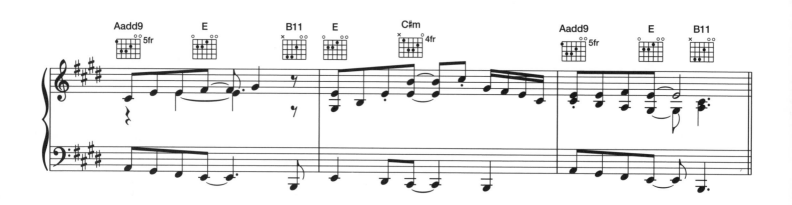

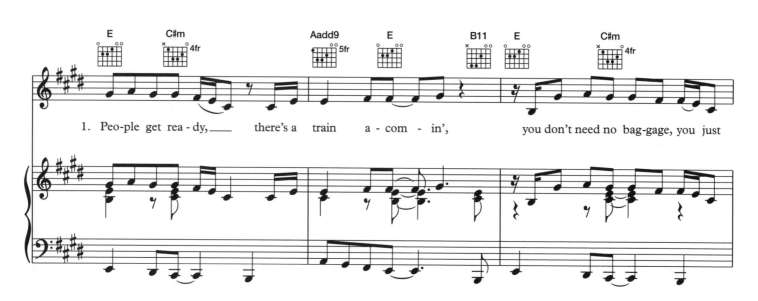

1. Peo-ple get rea-dy,___ there's a train a-com-in', you don't need no bag-gage, you just

SONGBIRD

Words and Music by
Christine McVie

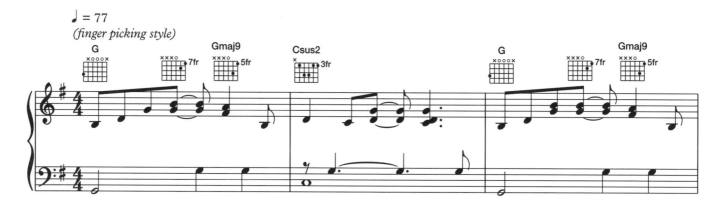

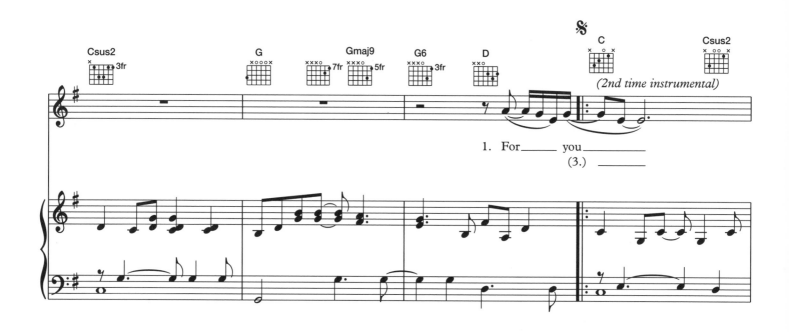

THEY CALL IT STORMY MONDAY

Words and Music by
Aaron 'T–Bone' Walker

WAY BEYOND THE BLUE

Traditional

WHAT A WONDERFUL WORLD

Words and Music by
George Weiss and Bob Thiele

TIME AFTER TIME

Words and Music by
Robert Hyman and Cyndi Lauper

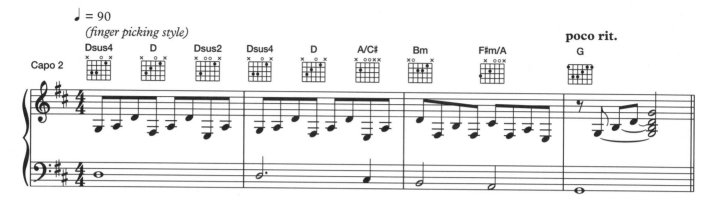

1. Ly - ing in — my bed — I hear — the clock — tick and think — of you. — Turn - ing in — cir - cles, — con -

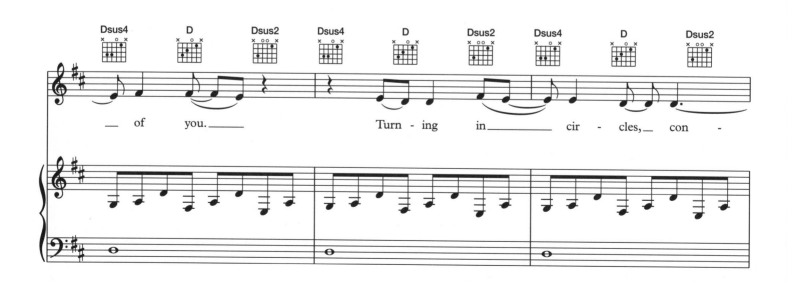